Jayden
and the
Sack of Fish

Marcia Hughes

ISBN 979-8-88832-825-5 (paperback)
ISBN 979-8-88832-826-2 (digital)

Christian Faith Publishing
832 Park Avenue
Meadville, PA 16335
www.christianfaithpublishing.com

Printed in the United States of America

With All My Love G. G.

Each year in the spring, shortly after his birthday, Jayden was sent to stay with his grandparents for vacation. They lived on one of the many islands, located a few miles offshore from the Main Land. Jayden called his grandparents Granny and Pap-Pap. Granny and Pap-Pap lived on the largest of these beautiful islands. They lived in a big wood and stone house called the Family House. It was where Jayden's mother lived when she was a child. Many of Jayden's aunts, uncles, and cousins all lived in the house at some time. Now most of the family had moved away, like his mom and dad, to go live and work on the Main Land.

The island is modern like the Main Land except some of the old ways still existed. Fortunately, Granny and Pap-Pap had a modern home. Granny had a beautiful electric stove and refrigerator. Pap-Pap drove a nice car that he was always working on to keep it clean and shiny. There are paved wide roads and narrow roads made of dirt mixed with gravel on the island. All of these roads were lined with tall palm trees topped with yummy coconuts hidden among dark green leaves. There are also shrubs and vines of many colors that grow all over the island. These colorful plants gave the entire island a storybook quality. Everywhere you look, there are green plants, purple plants, and white, yellow, red, blue, and lilac plants. To Jayden, going to the island was like stepping into another world.

The island has every kind of vehicle too. There are the modern vehicles that the vacationers usually drive. And the other older vehicles like trucks, bicycles, buses, and cars tend to belong to the permanent residents of the island. But Jayden's favorite vehicles are the horse-drawn wagons. He loved watching the team of giant horses pulling big wagons filled with supplies. Horses like that didn't exist on the Main Land where he lived.

One day, after getting permission from its owner, Pap-Pap was allowed to let three-year-old Jayden give an apple to Old Joe. Old Joe was a big brown horse with a long white mane and furry feet. Pap-Pap called the fur around Old Joe's feet feathers. Jayden's hand trembled a little as he gave Old Joe the apple. But he was elated to feed the horse.

After that, Pap-Pap held Jayden high in the air so that he could pat Old Joe on his shoulder. That was just one of many happy days spent on the island. There was always something interesting and exciting like that to do while spending the summer with his grandparents.

As Pap-Pap and Jayden walked home that day, Pap-Pap told Jayden about the celebration of the island tradition. Part of the tradition had to do with children over four years of age and under seven running to the shore to collect fish to feed their families. This was something Jayden truly wanted to do.

Once hearing of this, he practiced running as often as he could. He ran around the outside of his grandparents' house like a dog chasing his tail, several times a day. Around and around, he would go until his legs became so tired that he dropped to the grass-covered ground. As he sat in the cool, lush, sweet-smelling green grass, looking up at the many white fluffy clouds that lazily floated across the sky, he thought about his special day. He pictured himself carrying a giant sack of fish on his back. He was confident; when the day came, he would bring back lots and lots of fish for Granny and Pap-Pap.

After leaving Granny and Pap-Pap's house last year and returning to the Main Land with his mom and dad, the thought of the tradition screamed in his head. Jayden's mom and dad took him to the park not far from where they lived often to practice running so his legs would be strong and ready to participate in the tradition. Jayden's mom and dad had both participated in the tradition when they were children. With each practice, Jayden was able to run faster and for a longer time. He wanted to be known as the fastest kid on the island.

Jayden, Age Four

Now at age four, Jayden was anxiously looking forward to staying with his grandparents again. He had been told last year, when he was three years old, about a yearly celebration of the tradition that took place on the island. The main tradition was that the children between the ages of four and seven were expected to run to the shore and bring back a sack filled with fish. At this age, children all over the island demonstrated that they were old enough to help feed their families if needed. The rest of the tradition was that when the boats came back from the sea filled with fish, it was time to feast and celebrate. This was an old tradition on the island still practiced in these modern times. It's one of those traditions that was symbolically honored but not needed. Most people did it for the fun, the celebration, and the excitement.

On the day that the boats returned from the sea, the delicious aroma of cooked food could be smelled, coming from all over the island, signaling this wonderful event. Colorful ribbons and balloons would be used to decorate everything on the island. Men, women, and children would wear scarves or bandanas of many colors. As people unload the fish from the boats, they would sing a traditional song that went something like this, "The boats are in, go grab a friend, to help unload the boats!" These words were repeated over and over again and again to this day.

The year Jayden was away from the big island had been long, but finally, he was traveling on the ferry boat with his parents to stay with Granny and Pap-Pap once again. When he got to Granny and Pa-Pa's house, he happily received welcoming hugs and kisses from both. He then said the usual tearful goodbyes to his mom and dad, and off he went running into the Family House. He knew there would not be much time before he was to run to the shore and fill his sack with fish. That was all he could think about. He believed he had a lot to do before then.

That very night, his grandparents told him that the fishing boats had been seen way offshore. This meant that they would be arriving soon. In less than a day's time, he would be running as fast as he could toward the shore. The excitement of it all was unbearable. Jayden was unable to stop himself from running and jumping all over the place. He was extremely eager to get started with his run to the shore.

Granny kept him busy by having him gather what he would need for his journey. He was given a burlap sack containing a canister of water, a hunk of cheese, and some of Granny's delicious homemade bread. Jayden placed the sack of food and water near his bed, along with his fastest red-and-white running shoes. Unbeknownst to Jayden, his Pap-Pap would discreetly follow him to the shore to keep him safe.

Still eager to get started, Jayden paced in and out of the house. It was a beautiful warm summer starlit night. Granny had just finished cleaning the kitchen when she noticed Jayden pacing. She calmly encouraged him to save his strength for the run. He took her advice and went to bed. Surprisingly, as soon as his head hit the pillow, he fell asleep. Granny had gone to bed soon after Jayden and slept too.

Within what seemed like moments, she was awakened by the sound of bells ringing, trucks tooting their horns, and carts creaking along the dirt and gravel road that ran near the Family House. There were also horses stomping their feet and snorting loudly while pulling wagons filled with big chunks of ice to keep the fish fresh, heading to the shore. The sound of villagers' voices could be heard above all else yelling, "The boats are in! The boats are in!"

The fishing boats were in, and everyone was on the move. The path that Jayden and the other children would take to the shore ran beside the road filled with vehicles. Jayden had been warned to stay on the path and not go onto the road because he could be knocked down by vehicles and people running. And besides, Granny thought, Pap-Pap would be there to keep Jayden safe.

Quickly, Granny got up and placed her bare feet into her comfortable slippers. She rushed to Jayden's room and found him still asleep. Gently she shook him and calmly informed him that it was time to get up. Drowsily, he sat up. It took him a moment to realize that it was time for him to run to the shore. As if energized by lightning, Jayden suddenly jumped out of bed, saying over and over, "It's time! It's time!"

Possessed by this notion, he ran past Granny, through the kitchen, and onto the porch. Granny had run out of her comfortable slippers in an attempt to keep up with him. She caught him before he went any farther. Upon doing so, she begged him to stop and come back into the house. He saw her looking at his bare feet and then hers. He noticed that neither Granny nor he had on any shoes. They both laughed at the sight of their bare feet and went back into the house. He realized that he had forgotten to put on his fastest red-and-white shoes and grab his burlap sack. He also had not bothered to wash up or brush his teeth. Most of all, he would need to eat breakfast to have the energy to run the one mile that it took to get to the shore and the one mile back home. Granny reminded him of these things in her calm gentle way. She also reminded him that the tradition was all about how well you do, not how fast.

With Granny's help, Jayden did everything he needed to do before starting his journey. He cooperated with Granny but never calmed down. He put on his fast shoes and grabbed his burlap sack. As soon as Granny finished inspecting him to make sure he had everything he needed, he ran like the wind, out of the kitchen and onto the porch. With the agility of a mountain goat, he leaped down the two little steps of the porch and onto the stone road. While heading toward the designated path, he was heard yelling, "Goodbye, Granny! Goodbye, Granny!"

Granny stood on the porch and waved goodbye as she watched her little fellow disappear down the path. After she could no longer see him, she remained standing and staring in his direction, eyes glistening with emotion. She smiled when she saw Pap-Pap trying to keep a close eye on their grandson without being noticed. She knew that Jayden would be safe and do well. There was always someone at the shore to see to it that the children who participated in honoring the tradition would have plenty of fish to fill their burlap sacks.

With a few stops in between for resting and sipping water, Jayden had successfully reached the shore in record time. Exhausted and thirsty, he sat on one of the many boulders that littered the shore and took big gulps of water from the canister that he had quickly removed from his sack. The sun was very bright, which made running a hot and sweaty task. Granny told him not to get any closer to the shore than the rocks and boulders. He sat on a big boulder and waited until the children from other families arrived.

They had not been far behind. Finding their own boulders near Jayden, they sat down exhausted. Eagerly reaching into burlap sacks, they grabbed what each had brought. Hungrily, they began eating and drinking. All of that running had given everyone a ravenous appetite. Some had bread and cheese like Jayden. Others had a hunk of ham to go with their bread. After eating, they sipped on what was left of their water and quietly talked among themselves while resting.

As they did so, a man with a huge burlap sack slung over one shoulder that weighed him down approached. The man was bent almost in half with the weight of the big heavy sack. The children all watched as, without a word, the man placed the sack on the ground in front of them and untied the rope that held it together.

They all stared, eyes wide, as fish of all kinds fell out of the man's huge sack. There were big red fishes, medium yellow fishes, and little fishes, each a different color of the rainbow. There were also things in that sack that some of the children had never seen before. Something with long tentacles slithered away beneath the fish.

Before the sight of these live fish, Jayden had only seen fish cooked and on his plate. These fish were flopping around. The children were hesitant to move toward the fish until the man who had a deep gravelly voice said, "What are you waiting for? Grab your fish and go. Nothing there will harm you. I have things to do." Earlier, the man had made sure all of the fishes in his sack were harmless.

In an instant, they picked up their empty burlap sacks. The man laughed out loud as he watched the children go after the fish. Pap-pap, who had been watching from a distance, laughed too. The children were slipping and sliding all over the place, as they tried to get fish into their sacks. They were amazed to see that the fish were so surprisingly slippery.

Soon, they all had finally gotten some fish into their burlap sacks along with their empty water canisters. The man with the gravelly voice tied each little sack tight and sent the children on their way. With a one-mile walk looming before them and a heavy sack of fish slung over their shoulder, they knew it would be a long journey. But all of the children were determined to complete the tradition. Jayden and the other children began their journey home by planting one foot in front of the other. The food they had eaten and the water they had drank gave each child a needed boost of energy. It was enough energy to get all of the children home.

As Pap-Pap discretely followed, watching Jayden from the edge of the road, he noticed other parents were doing the same. The sound of celebrating could be heard coming from every direction. It was a wonderful and happy sound.

Soon, with the weight of the heavy sack of fish slung over his shoulder, huffing and puffing from exhaustion, rivulets of dirty sweat running down his face, after a time, he heard his family cheering and applauding. He raised his head and saw Granny watching proudly as she dabbed at her eyes once again with a tissue. Pap-Pap had gone past Jayden without being noticed and was there too, along with other family members who still lived on the island. Everyone continued to cheer as Jayden smiled and proudly opened his sack to display all of the fish he had brought back from the shore. Jayden felt the pride of a warrior who had come home a weary hero.

The end!

Written by Marcia Hughes

About the Author

Marcia Hughes attended the Community College of Allegheny County where she obtained some knowledge of creative writing. She has lived in Pittsburgh, Pennsylvania, for the past seventy years. The completion of this story is part of her bucket list. It will also serve as a legacy to her great-grandson Jayden.